DEVIL'S NOSE

DEVIL'S NOSE

*Overboard in Lake
Ontario #2*

CAROL OSCHMANN

Carol Oschmann

CONTENTS

Copyright — vii
Dedication — ix
Prologue — xi

One — 1

Two — 7

Three — 13

Four — 15

Five — 21

Six — 25

Seven — 31

Eight — 37

Nine
43

Ten
49

Eleven
53

Twelve
57

Thirteen
63

Fourteen
69

Fifteen
73

Sixteen
79

Seventeen
81

Notes and Author's Other Books
89

Copyright 2023 by Carol Oschmann

First printing 2023

Many thanks to Jerry Fisher of Kent, NY for his beautiful cover photo of Devil's Nose.
Also, thanks to Linda Chamberlain of Brockport, NY for her great job of editing.

Devil's Nose is a well known landmark at the west end of Hamlin Beach State park, NY. It's on the south shore of Lake Ontario, the smallest of the Great Lakes. The Great Lakes have provided much enjoyment for boaters, fishermen, and nature lovers. It will provide joy for many years to come. This book is dedicated to all those people who wish to be able to enjoy the beauty of it's waters.

Fifteen-year-old Tom ducked as bullets sailed over his head. What the heck? Shaking fearfully, he hid behind a big chestnut tree to see where they had come from. It wasn't hunting season. For a second, it was quiet, and then the bullets started flying again. Had they seen him? No, this time, the shots seemed to be going in a different direction, growing fainter as if the gunman was moving away from him.

Then he saw someone hiding behind a big rock. He couldn't remember a rock that big on this hiking trail at the top of Devil's Nose. Then, he saw a man, also hiding from the shooter and the bullets. He wore a German uniform and one of those thick cereal bowl helmets. A Nazi? "I must be dreaming," thought Tom. He saw the man run and throw something into the lake. "I've got to wake myself up."

Just then, the Nazi turned and saw Tom He shouted at Tom! "Get out of my dream!"

Tom laughed as he rolled out of bed. Mrs. Parsons said that when God gives you something to laugh at in your dream, it's like a reward for doing something right. He'd been trying as he worked hard to make himself needed at the marina.

CHAPTER ONE

Tom slid out of his bed and onto the deck. He was back sleeping on the Playhouse, his Uncle BJ's houseboat. Last year, during boating season, they had lived on it. That was before winning the big house on the hill in a negotiated deal with the owner.

The nosy neighbor made his jail sentence easier by giving up his house to them. He wasn't a killer; he got involved with some of them. That was also just before BJ (his uncle) and Cindy married.

Tom groaned and ran his fingers through his dark brown curly hair as he fought with himself. Should I stay up or go back to sleep? He climbed the few steps to the galley, turning the lights on. The clock said two am. Back to sleep, for sure, but first, I've got to get out of this dream! He searched the cupboards for cereal, a slice of bread, anything to return to this world. No luck. Everything was up at the big house.

He chuckled again as he remembered his dream with the Nazi saying, "Get out of my dream!" "It was my dream," Tom silently argued.

"I might as well sit out on the deck and look at the lake and the sky. At least the winds and waves are calm, the stars bright. A nice warm night to sit outside."

Tom thought that if it stayed this way, he could take his sailing class out on the lake instead of the Genesee River. There were wide open spaces to sail in Lake Ontario.

Since it was a weekday, few boaters would likely be out. Maybe some Coast Guard Auxiliary boats with retired skippers would rope off his territory. They'd watch students who got too close to being blown off course. Tom thought of the group of retirees who often helped out that way.

He laughed when he thought of the only time his parents took out the little two-person Sunfish sailboat. They struggled to go one way while the wind carried them another. Tom, only twelve then, got the little motorboat out and saved them. He teased them about having a race with the house, and the house was winning.

He spoke to them in heaven, "I wish you were here so I could still tease you,"

He gazed along the shoreline as far as Devil's Nose. It blocked his view. Startled, he rushed inside to get the binoculars. He swore he saw lights there. Nothing now, but I saw what I saw, he thought.

He settled back down on the deck to keep watch. He thought about his dream. Was someone really there doing something illegal? His other dreams had predicted the future.

He'd seen the marina water on fire with a gas slick that the people in the abandoned hotel had inadvertently spilled. He needed to save them and protect the boats, which he managed to do. In his dream, it had been aliens, like ET, but in life, they turned out to be aliens smuggled from across the lake in Canada to hide in the old hotel across the way.

It was all burned down now, thought Tom, remembering the illegal aliens who'd started the fire to keep warm. Many had jumped out the holes in the walls, only to be picked up by boaters, loaded on school buses, and taken to government shelters.

This dream, tonight, was way in the past, World War II. I wasn't even born; my parents weren't even born then, thought Tom. Maybe Grandma. Finally, he fell back asleep with no dreams.

"Tom!" BJ was shaking him awake. "You're due at the Coast Guard Station in two hours. Better get up to the house, get cleaned up, and have breakfast. I'll drive you there. Call me when you're done, or catch a ride on the Coast Guard 44cutter when they make their rounds." Tom jumped up to do as he was told.

"I almost didn't see you on this side of the boat," BJ added.

"I'm sorry," Tom said. "I had a dream that woke me up. I guess I fell back asleep here after seeing lights at the base of Devil's Nose."

"Lights? In the middle of the night?"

"A little after two am, to be exact," Tom said.

"I'll call the park office about it. Get going! You don't want to be late." Tom knew BJ would call. They'd been through a lot together, and Tom knew that BJ would never doubt his word.

"Meet you at the car in half an hour!"

*****

Tom gazed at the shore from the aft deck of the Coast Guard 44Cutter. What a way to go home from work, he smiled.

Seaman Gary stepped over some coiled-up line to shout to Tom over the noise of the engines. "How'd the class go today?"

Tom gave a thumbs up.

"Want to try some handicapped kids next week on Tuesday?"

"I've never dealt with someone with a physical disability," Tom shouted. "I'm game if someone who knows them can be by my side."

"We can arrange that. This group has more mental rather than physical disabilities."

"Oh, just like me," joked Tom. That wasn't the right thing to say, he thought. Then, he changed the subject. "I never tire of watching the shoreline. We passed Ontario Beach Park, and next will be Braddock's Bay. What a different view one gets from out here!"

"That reminds me," Gary shouted, "the municipal marina there has lost its caretakers. Can you and BJ help us with it until we find new people?"

"I'll ask BJ. We could use the money. It wouldn't be far from my cousin Sara."

"There's a small cottage on the property where someone could stay overnight when it's busy, like a holiday weekend. Need someone to launch boats, pump gas, assign docks, that sort of thing."

"If only I was old enough to stay by myself. I'm looking forward to getting my driver's license, but before that, I'll be doing some diving. But we'll have time to help at a second marina. We have good help at BJ's Marina."

"Lots of luck with the diving! There's not much to see in these waters. Where do you plan to dive?"

Tom felt a chill up his spine. Should I keep it to myself? He wondered. But Seaman Gary was friendly, and he'd been with the Coast Guard a long time. "I'm thinking of the area around the base of Devil's Nose."

All of a sudden, Seaman Gary stiffened up. "Why would you want to go there? It's a dangerous area, with lots of table rocks to get stuck on. Stay away from there!" He turned back to the helm to talk to his crew.

I know that, thought Tom. It was nice of Gary to warn me away, or was it? After last year, even the sheriff was not to be trusted. I have to think this over. Glad I didn't say I saw something in a dream.

What if some Nazi threw something in the water at the base of Devil's Nose? I need to know what it was. But then again, how would a person in full Nazi uniform get to Devil's Nose? One more of life's puzzles. What did BJ discover about those lights I saw this morning?

Tom surveyed the 44 cutter. It was a nice wide open boat, forty-four feet long, fits into our harbor. It's tough and ready for towing disabled vessels. They say it could roll over in a bad storm with high waves and still be safe.

I don't want to try that out. He saw some diving gear and wondered how often they used that. I'd like to get them to dive at the base of Devil's Nose. Better keep it to myself. People might think I'm crazy if they knew about my dreams.

Thinking of the boat's dive gear, there's not much for them to dive for unless someone drops their outboard motor. That's happened a few times.

He remembered when that outboard motorboat was sinking outside Oak Orchard River. The owner was frantic about saving his motor and boat. BJ jumped in the water, hooked some lines around the boat while I handled the marina's work boat, towed it right up. I caught on fast to handling BJ's work boat, the Dutch Tug, Tom mused. Hope driving a car on the open road is just as easy. BJ dried out the motor, and it was as good as new. And the guy blustered over paying us. People!

I've gone down a few times to save a phone or camera, thought Tom. I've got the knowledge and the gear. Now, to have a few more of those dreams so I know where to look. Tom couldn't believe he wanted more dreams like last night, with bullets whistling over his head. It had to be someplace in Germany or France, and I will likely not get there.

While lost in his thoughts, Tom looked up and realized that they'd just passed Devil's Nose and were pulling into BJ's Marina. Home, again.

CHAPTER TWO

Cary, Tom's classmate, and Nina, one of the other people who ran away from the foster home at the farm last year, greeted Tom as he climbed off the 44Cutter. They both helped out at the marina as they lived close by.

He greeted them both with a wide grin. Cary wore the jeans and t-shirt Cindy had helped him pick out for her birthday last year. The rosy pink looked great with her straight brown hair. She'd worn it almost every day to school last year and often to work at the marina this summer. I got good taste, he told himself. In clothes and girls. Course they had practically been thrown together.

They had shared last year's excitement, the burned-down old hotel at the end of County Line Rd. There was the murder of the crooked sheriff and more. Plus, her father was one of Tom's guardians, so he was allowed to stay with his (then) single uncle.

The smugglers brought the immigrants in by boat from across the lake, in Canada, at night when no one was looking. They led them through the pilings that held up the old hotel, to the trap door in the floor.

Farm buses picked them up and took them to the farm where Tom and Nina stayed. It was dangerous for both of them, and they ran away in different directions. Nina to another county. Tom ran to the old hotel, then to his uncle's marina.

He didn't realize smugglers were using the place until the fire started. By then, Tom was safe – sort of – on the other side of the marina.

That explained why BJ's Marina was in jeopardy: Tom's very life. The smugglers wanted to own the marina to continue their activities without anyone watching them.

"Hi!" both girls eagerly greeted Tom."BJ's in the office and wants to talk to you," Cary said. They all waved at the crew of the 44Cutter as it pulled away from the dock. Making a tight U-turn, pulling forward and back a bit until they were in the right direction and headed back out to the lake.

Tom took Cary's hand and headed to the office, where BJ had just hung up. It was a thing Tom did after last year. He sat on the end of a dock with Cary to watch the people hiding in the old hotel across the way. They had to pretend to be boyfriend and girlfriend having a romantic evening. They tried to tell each other jokes, sure they were being watched.

They reached the office. "I talked to the park manager," BJ said. "He sent some workers out to the base of Devil's Nose. They don't believe anyone was there. The usual stuff, stones, driftwood, and junk that could have washed up from the water. They didn't see any sign of campfires."

BJ wore a concerned look as he thought about the call. One could tell he and Tom were related. He was a lot like Tom's dad, only younger. He was often mistaken as Tom's older brother, with the same curly brown hair and an eagerness to get things done. He was taller than Tom. Tom was yet to have his growth spurt.

Cary called Tom shorty whenever she wanted to get him angry. Neither Tom nor BJ were quick to anger. Life brought enough of that on them, BJ had once said. They just put their heads together and tried to figure things out, like those lights Tom saw at the base of Devil's Nose.

"They wanted to know what you were doing up at that time of night? I don't think I made any friends with that call."

"Sorry," Tom answered. "I'll set my alarm tonight and see if I see the lights again. I didn't think it was a fire, more like a powerful lantern. Oh, I got some news. They want to start a Tuesday sailing class along with my Monday class for one thing."

Great!" looking at Tom's face, BJ guessed, "There's more?"

"The people running Braddock's Bay marina up and left. They asked if we could spend some hours there until they find new people?"

"If you girls stick around, we could take turns," BJ suggested. "You can go by boat, just don't stay too late. In case of an emergency, we can put a sign on the office door stating our hours and this phone number."

Tom replied, "I wish I had my driver's license."

"Yeah, I know. You'll have it shortly. You already drive everything in this marina."

The girls were whispering in the corner. Then, they seemed to come to a decision. Cary said, "I'll have to ask my father, but we're both willing. The added hours here will help with some new clothes for school."

Tom groaned, "Not thinking of that already!" Nina stuck her tongue out at Tom. He laughed, but that was why he wanted the job at the bay. The government paid well.

"I'll call Chief Garret and talk it over with him after I talk to Judge Travers. I'm sure we can work something out." Just then, a horn honked, and Cary ran out to pump somebody's gas for their boat. "Let's get to work, we've got some grass to cut and a boat to launch."

"I'll cut the grass," Nina offered.

"I'll help with the boat," Tom said. Soon, no one was in the office.

And the phone started ringing. The machine picked up the message, "Keep your noses out of things at Devil's Nose!"

*****

Tom had an appointment with his counselor, Mrs Parsons. She stopped by the marina at four, and she and Tom met privately at the Playhouse. "How are things going," she asked.

"Great," Tom replied. "I taught a class in sailing for the Coast Guard this morning. They asked me to do another class for mentally disabled kids."

"Sounds like they like the job you're doing. Those mentally disabled kids can be smarter than they look. They might take to sailing a boat, you never know. It would give them a feeling of power they probably don't have. It's nice to broaden what they think of themselves and what they can do. Any dreams?"

"Yeah," said Tom. He then told her of being at the top of Devil's Nose and someone shooting a gun, maybe at him. He ducked behind a tree and saw a Nazi soldier hiding from the gunman. "That happened just last night. Then I got up, sat on the deck facing the Nose, and saw lights at the base. Two o'clock in the morning."

"I sure don't know what to make of that. Sounds like someone should look into those lights. Like the other dreams, maybe the dream is a matter of wait and see."

"I laughed my way up to the deck and sat out to see the Nose. I remember you saying when God gives you something to laugh at in your dreams, it most likely means you did something right."

"From the reports that I get from Cary's dad, Judge Travers, you are doing really good."

Tom couldn't shake away the dream. "But why a German soldier, though?" He asked. "I'll probably never run into one of them unless I take up traveling, and that's not likely."

"You only know what the future holds once it gets here. Speaking of German soldiers, have you visited the Prisoner Of War Camp on the other side of Hamlin Beach?"

"I didn't know there was one," Tom replied.

"You might want to visit it. It might hold some answers to your dream. In World War II, it was a place to house prisoners of war. The story is that they were let out to work in the fields for the farmers. There was a shortage of farm workers, with many farm boys joining the services to fight for our country.

"Before that," she continued, "it was a CCC camp, Civilian Conservation Corps, set up to provide housing for the young fellows who built the park, 1935 to 1941. It became a POW camp housing German prisoners of war from 1944 to 1946."

"Sounds like a question that might come up in school. Was it a president that started the Civilian Conservation Corps?"

"President Theodore Roosevelt. You going to keep all this stuff in your head?"

"I'm pretty good with things that interest me."

"Well, many of the POWs worked in Duffy Mott."

"The canning factory?"

"The same. Some of your family might have worked there also. It's gone now."

"Gram worked there. I've got to check her old house down the road. She kept a diary. I might learn some neat things there. I'll go through her old pictures, too. I've got so much I want to do. I want to go diving at the base of the Nose, see if I see anything someone might have thrown in."

"You won't go alone!"

"No, Cary can dive also, so the two of us will have a nice day exploring around the table rocks at the base if I can find the time.

"Be sure to let BJ know what you're doing. I've heard tough things about those table rocks."

"We ensure every boater knows to go way out when approaching the Nose. I've seen too many propellers lost there because someone didn't go out far enough."

"If I remember my history, there were several big shipwrecks in the 1700's there. And the Nose used to be eighty feet high."

"It's all sand and has been eroding over the years. How did those big, flat, solid rocks get there from a sand hill?"

"Another good question to research if you ever have time."

Tom giggled. "Maybe when school starts, if I remember, I could use it for a research paper if some teacher assigns one."

"Anything else?" Mrs. Parson wanted to know.

"We've been asked to keep the marina at Braddock's Bay open until the state finds new people to run it."

"You will be busy this summer. Talk about running. I've got to get back home and get dinner going. See you in a month. Stay safe if you do those dives! Love that dream. Call me with updates; you've got me curious now."

Tom walked her out to her car. He was thinking how last year they'd become good friends. He didn't mind seeing a counselor, especially when she could stop by the marina on her way home from work, and she likes to talk dreams. Sometimes, she can figure them out. She doesn't think I'm crazy for having them, unlike that person at the park office.

"Tom!" shouted BJ. "Wait up. You and I will go to Braddock's Bay Marina tomorrow; look the situation over."

"Tomorrow's Tuesday. We should be slow here."

"The girls will be here, along with Judge Travers, and we'll just be a phone call away."

"That's nice of Cary's dad to come and help."

"Nothing better to do when you're retired than hang out on your boat."

"Oh yeah, how could I forget about the Candy Kiss?"

CHAPTER THREE

It stayed light out, til almost nine. Tom told BJ he was taking a bike ride to Gram's house to look for some papers. That was home for Tom until Gram passed away last year and the state decided Tom had to go into a foster care at the farm.

The decision was that BJ being young and single himself, could not provide a good environment for Tom. Before all that, BJ spent his summers on the Playhouse, his houseboat, and winters at Gram's. Tom was often at the marina helping out. After the sheriff got murdered, the court decided he could stay at the marina. Judge Travers would be taking partial responsibility for Tom.

Tom jumped on his bike and headed south on County-Line Rd. It wasn't even a mile. Tom stood in the front yard looking up at his old bedroom windows with longing. He loved the marina, no place he'd rather be. However, the memories of Gram and his parents when they were alive still bothered him.

He went around to the back door and parked his bike out of sight of the road. Last time he was here, he was afraid of ghosts. He hadn't found ghosts but real live bad guys. He pulled himself up straight, he wasn't that young, anymore.

He climbed the steps, crossed the porch and inserted the key in the back door. It opened onto the kitchen and Tom felt for the light switch. He was shocked to see someone had been there again. "We had the locks changed, after we learned the smugglers were using this place for meetings. Who was here now?"

No doubt, no one was here, at the moment. "We need to take time to empty the place out and get it ready for sale," Tom thought. Then we won't have these break-ins to worry about.

He went straight to Gram's bedroom, just off the living room. Gram always kept a diary. If I can find that diary, there may be more than one, probably a stack. I need to go back to 1944, and her time working at Duffy Mott. I can spend my empty time reading forward. It will be interesting to read what her life was like. Maybe I can talk Cary and Nina into reading some of it and telling me about it.

In the back of a closet, Tom found a stack of diaries that went back to 1955. Not far enough. On a second bit of inspiration, he went up to the attic, and found what he wanted. Her favorite trunk was hidden under some other things in a corner where the roof came down and met the floor. It was all he could do to fit in there. Maybe it was still there because no one thought it was worth while to struggle under that corner of roof. Whoever has been in here might be back. I've got to see what the Judge and BJ can do about this.

Gram had been very neat but it wasn't neat now. It looked like people were going through her things. Glad they didn't find the diaries. I'll have to see how many I can hold on the bike. I'll find 1944 and grab as many around that date as I can carry. I can come back later for the rest, maybe get BJ here with the truck. But I want to start reading them tonight. Tomorrow we start at Braddock's Bay Marina.

CHAPTER FOUR

BJ and Tom sifted through the various piles of paperwork left behind at the bay's marina. "Well, the first thing that I see, besides taking money from the day launchers, is to get a map made up of the docks. We need to start assigning spaces. This seems to be a list of last years dockers. Let's see if we can fit them in where they were last year," BJ said.

Tom got a huge piece of plain paper and started drawing the docking system. He had to go outside a few times to refresh his memory. "Should I make sure the larger boats, and the sailboats that have a deep keel are on the end docks?" Tom asked.

"We'll follow last year's as close as we can. We need to leave some open spaces for new people. We don't know for sure that everyone will come back yet." Tom had a job ahead of him. He walked the docks a few times to find that one section had to be entirely for smaller boats or boats with a deep inboard motor like a Penn Yan. They can go in much shallower water. The water isn't very deep here, he realized.

BJ began going through the receipts to see who had already paid for a dock for this year. Customers kept knocking on the door to the office to see where they should go, or pay for a dock.

"My boy, Tom, is out on the docks now. He'll let you know where you'll be as soon as he figures it all out. It's a little hard to follow the notes we have from last year." BJ repeated that over and over. The day went fast and soon they were hanging a closed sign on the door with instructions that they'd be back tomorrow.

"How about we grab a hot dog at Schaller's?" BJ suggested.

"You don't have to ask me, I'll go there anytime. That's a plus for working here! If I'm here alone, I wonder if they deliver."

"We'll ask when we get there."

"BJ, there's one name on the old list that's kind of infamous."

"Yeah, I noticed, 'Sam Sanders'. Let's see what he's like. If he causes any trouble, we'll deal with him just like any other person. I'm sure he values his boat and the time to get away from everything."

"That's the guy that's supposed to be mafia, isn't he?"

"Just treat him like any other boater. We probably won't see him much."

*****

On their way back home BJ had a bright idea. "Let's take the roads close to the lake and we can stop and visit the POW Camp you've been talking about."

"Gee, thanks. I've been hoping to find some clues to my dream there."

BJ drove the Parkway to Brockport Yacht Club, got off, and picked up the beginning of Moscow road so they wouldn't miss the small sign for the POW Camp. They found it! They pulled in the long driveway and found a man working on another sign, installing some new brochures, it seemed. Just in time, Tom took one.

"Would you like to take a tour? We've got it mostly laid out so you can follow the map in the brochure. We found the boundaries of the camp by using a metal detector and then followed the part of the fencing that was buried underground. There was one guard tower right here."

Tom was curious to know, "Did they have any breakouts and have to shoot any prisoners?"

"We don't know a lot about the camp. A lot of the prisoners helped out at area farms or worked at Duffy Mott. Ever hear of that?"

"Yes, my Grandmother worked there. She never said anything about German prisoners of war."

"They were welcome on the farms. A lot of farm boys had to serve in the war leaving the farms short-handed. The farmers' wives cooked for them and treated them like family. So I would imagine they had a decent life being so far from home and not sure if they'd even get to go back.

"Did they get paid for their work?" BJ asked

"They got paid in coupons that they traded at the camp store. They could buy things like candy, cigarettes and soap. One soldier came back after we started to clear the land here and stake out the boundaries, barracks and such. He showed us a wallet he bought in the store."

Tom asked, "Are you sure there was never a breakout? I assume the guards stood up high with guns for a reason."

"Now that you mention it, there was one fellow who robbed the store and escaped, but they got him at the other end of the park, near Devil's Nose. They never found what he stole and he wouldn't say. Can't imagine they had any money in the store."

BJ turned to Tom, "It's dinner time for this fellow. Let's come back when we have more time. This is a very interesting bit of history and right in our own backyard." Tom agreed and they headed towards home.

"Have any more dreams about that?"

"No, maybe tonight since we visited here. Did you call Cindy to let her know we're on our way home and had supper without her?" Tom wanted to know. Life was truly better for the two bachelors since Cindy came into their lives and especially since BJ married her last year. Tom had no more doubts that he was welcome at BJ's marina.

"She's fine with that. She did say there was a strange message on our answering machine. She said it was something about keeping our noses away from Devil's Nose. I think you're onto something."

"I can't wait to do some diving there."

"I just might join you."

"That would be great. I found some strange things at Gram's house last night. I think we'd better find time to clean it out and put it up for sale."

"You okay with that?" BJ asked. Tom glanced at BJ to see a wetness around his eyes. Selling the old house bothered him? More than Tom realized. It was his grandmother, but BJ's mom. Of course, he'd want to hold onto it. I should have thought of that before I blurted that out.

"Yes, but it's up to you. Someone has been in there again. I was able to get the diaries I wanted, but we should save all of them. It's history."

"Okay, maybe Mrs. Travers or Cindy will have some ideas on how to begin that process, but you're right. We need to take that one worry off our hands! And when we sell it, we can put the money aside for you for college."

No!" said Tom dramatically. "I'm not through with high school and who needs a college education to run a marina?" Tom joked, probably getting himself into hot water again. BJ hadn't been able to go to college.

"You never know where the future will take you," BJ joked back. "I heard you said something about going to Europe."

"You were listening in to my conversation with my counselor, Mrs. Parsons!"

BJ laughed, "She has to give me the highlights of your talks. I'm your parent, now. Besides, we'll sell it so it does some good instead of sitting there and rotting. Maybe a family with little children will move in. That would be fun. If you go to college, you'll have money to pay for schooling and a good job to build your own new house."

"I'm putting my bid in, right now, for Judge Traver's property where the old hotel burned down."

"Might have to fight Cary for that bit of land."

They pulled into the driveway of the big house they now called home, across the street from the marina. "Let's say hello and then walk down to the office and listen to that message."

CHAPTER FIVE

The next couple of weeks were busy, getting the boaters assigned to docks at both marinas. Tom seemed to spend most of his time at Braddock's Bay.

They'd mentioned their idea of cleaning up Gram's house and putting it on the market with Cindy. She said she'd talk to Mrs. Travers. See what the two of them could come up with.

This day was not a good one. One man didn't like the dock Tom assigned him and proceeded to call him all kinds of names. The guy was livid, beyond belief or reason. With clenched fists, he declared he was going to call the town supervisor and raise trouble for them. He said they needed to get someone in there who knew what they were doing!

After he left Tom called BJ, almost in tears, asked if he could make a run down there and handle this docker.

Another man stood waiting and obviously felt sorry for Tom. He said not to worry. He would talk to the guy.

"What dock is he supposed to be on?" Tom told him and wondered who he was.

Another man, waiting patiently, said, "I think that guy will be sorry he crossed you."

"Why? Who is this guy?"

"Sam Sanders, you know who he is?"

"Yes," replied Tom. He felt a different kind of 'nervous' as he remembered he was the mafia guy.

BJ arrived to find the angry docker apologizing to Tom and saying the dock he assigned was just fine. BJ stayed back until the angry docker left.

"We have a new friend," Tom told BJ and proceeded to tell him who stepped in to solve the problem.

"Wow!" BJ said. He turned to go back to his own problems at his own marina when Sam Sanders walked back in the office.

"Thanks for helping out." BJ told him. "I'm Tom's Uncle."

"Yeah, I know. They call you BJ. Tom's doing a good job here. I'll be lazing on the boat, if he has any more problems, don't hesitate to share with me. A little talk, with my reputation, will go a long ways. Just leave a note on my boat if I'm not around." Sam said. "Do you have any hobbies besides running this marina?"

"I teach sailing to kids for the Coast Guard twice a week. And I sneak in a little diving when I can." Tom said.

"And he has a girlfriend," joked BJ.

Tom shot him a dirty look. "Watch out, BJ. I've got a new friend!" He indicated Sam.

They all laughed at that.

"What do you dive for?" Sam asked. "There were some ships wrecked back in the 1700's but they have probably been cleaned up by now. And you don't want to go near Devil's Nose. Those flat topped rocks can be dangerous in more ways than one."

BJ spoke up, "He's my man if someone loses a camera or wallet over the side of their boat."

"I didn't think of that. But I suppose it happens."

"More than one might think. We might as well call it a day. I can drive Tom home. Nice meeting you, and thanks for the help," BJ replied.

"See you around, kid."

"Bye, Sam," Tom replied. It seemed that was a second warning about Devil's Nose. "That's nice of him, but let's hope his way of handling things and ours are not to far different." Tom said with a sigh. BJ nodded in agreement.

They left the boat Tom had driven to work and climbed in BJ's truck.

"Am I getting paranoid or was that another warning about Devil's Nose?" Tom asked.

"Time will tell. I just might do some watching of the nose with you tonight. Got to get enough sleep though."

"We may not see much of the Nose. Did you notice the fog rolling in?" Tom asked.

"To tell you the truth, I haven't looked out at the lake because I was so busy worrying about you. Now that you mention it, I can see it coming in fast. The sun was shining earlier, lots of boats out on the lake today. I hope they've been more observant than I and gotten into a port."

"Amen to that. I wouldn't want to be out there and not be able to see anything, like another boat to crash into or my way home."

"I'm going to pick up speed and take a count of our boaters so we know whether to worry or not. We don't have to worry about Braddock's. They have navigational lights at the opening to the lake."

"Don't worry about speed, either. I know a good judge," joked Tom.

CHAPTER SIX

Back at the marina, BJ and Tom looked dismally out at what should have been Lake Ontario. The fog was so thick around them they had to walk from dock to dock to make sure the boats were all in. There were two missing, probably trying to find the mouth of the marina.

"Tom, drive the car onto the beach, very carefully, and lay on the horn. Maybe the sound will help them find home. I'm going into the office and monitor the radio and tell anyone out there to listen for the car horn."

"Good idea. I'm on it and I won't drive past the beach. First I'll pick up a handheld radio in case I need to talk to you."

"Do that. I trust you."

Tom got the handheld radio, got back in the truck and drove down to the beach, as close to the mouth of the marina as he could get. BJ gave him a signal from the office and then turned his attention to the first person calling for help in the fog.

"This is Rubber Ducky calling BJ's Marina."

"Rubber Ducky, switch and answer channel eighteen."

"BJ's marina, this is Curt aboard the Rubber Ducky. I've got a fishing party of four and we can't see our way to anything. We're headed south, according to the compass but can you help us find the channel to the marina?"

"Tom's on the beach in the car blowing the horn. Try and listen for that."

"The depth finder says we're in a hundred feet of water yet so maybe when we get closer to shore we'll hear it. Thanks. Too bad we can't get a light at the end of the jetties."

"Yeah, we tried but we're not a navigable waterway, so the army corps won't approve it. Best to stop talking and start listening, Captain."

"Rubber Ducky out for now."

"BJ's Marina switching and standing by on Channel 19."

The handheld radio beeped. "Yes Tom?"

"There's a sailboat coming in, all our sailboats are in. I'm afraid he's going to land on the beach. I tried reaching him on the handheld but I get nothing but silence."

"I'll notify the fire department, see if anyone's hanging around the station. We may need help if they miss the opening."

"Thanks. I got Cary honking the horn. Hope the battery doesn't run down. I'm going out on the beach, they're within shouting distance. I'll see if I can help. Maybe swim out to them if they get stuck. Tom out!"

BJ called the fire department. Soon he heard sirens coming down to the beach. The sirens were louder than the car horn; they also had bull horns. BJ relaxed a bit, until he got a call from his other missing boater.

"BJ's Marina, BJ's Marina. This is Wine Not calling BJ's marina."

"Wine not, Wine Not, This is BJ's Marina, switch and answer Channel Eighteen."

"BJ, just wanted you to know we're in the Oak Orchard River, tied up at the yacht club. We're fine, don't worry about us. But I did pick up some radio transmissions from a few other boats just as the fog was chasing us into port, so hang in there. Wine Not out."

"Thanks, Captain, BJ standing by on channel nineteen."

BJ took his other handheld radio and rushed up to the beach. The sailboat had a tall keel and ditched in about five feet of water, tipping to lie on its side. The firemen had gotten everyone off, waded them through the water to the beach. Cindy was offering to take them up to the house for some dry clothes and phone service. Tom was borrowing anchors from a few nearby boats to keep the sailboat in place and, hopefully, not rub too much on the rocks and sand under the shallow water.

Faintly, BJ heard another vessel calling. His boats were all accounted for. He raced to the office and the stronger radio and called them back. It would be a long evening, especially with guests in the house.

"BJ!" Hearing Cary's voice, BJ halted. "These people just followed the horns in. I put them on the gas dock. They live in Rochester and will be gone as soon as they can get rides into the city. They'll be back tomorrow for their boat. Just wanted to let you know, no problem!"

"Thanks, Cary. No problems!" He smiled as he left the cute teenager. Then he heard the car horn again and stopped short. He wondered who was honking the horn and remembered Nina, Cary's shadow as he liked to call her. It's nice to have such dedicated helpers but where was Cary's father, the judge? He was supposed to be sitting on his own sailboat today in case the girls needed him.

BJ stopped at Candy Kiss and found Judge Travers sound asleep. BJ shook his shoulder.

"What, what?"

"You're missing all the fun!" BJ hurriedly told him and pointed toward where the beach should be.

"Who took the world away?" The judge asked as he tried to see the beach and lake through the fog.

BJ laughed and hurried to the office where he heard another boater trying to make contact with land. Outside, he heard shouting and cheering as yet another boater came motoring through the opening to the lake.

"Where can I tie up?" he shouted. Judge Travers jumped up and indicated they could tie off his boat. Great, thought BJ. Another helping hand. Thank you God.

How are things going at the other marina in my charge, he wondered. He made a call to his new friend, Sam Sanders and found that the coast guard had moved in and taken charge.

He finally got to pick up the radio mic. "Boater in trouble, switch and answer BJ's Marina on channel eighteen, please." No one answered, Guess they found help or perhaps it was the boat that had just come in and tied to Candy Kiss.

This was an eventful day, Tom thought. Tomorrow we'll be dragging that sailboat off the rocks, accessing any damages and send it on its way. The boat's flags indicated Brockport Yacht Club. Not far from home. Maybe we'll get a repair out of it.

Cindy showed up with the large coffee pot and sandwiches. Tom pulled out the grill and some frozen burgers and rolls. Soon a small crowd, along with the firemen, gathered to talk about their adventures. They hoped no one else called on the marine radio.

To Tom's surprise, Seaman Gary was among the group from the sailboat. "Fancy meeting you here." Tom said. "What brings you to this part of the lake on a sailboat, no less, and you a skipper who couldn't find his way?"

"We were so busy looking at Devil's Nose, trying to see the erosion that's taken place over the winter, we didn't see the fog rolling in. Actually, the captain of the boat got the keel stuck between two table rocks. We got out, stood on the rocks, and pushed her off and jumped back in the boat. Those rocks are slippery and covered with sea weed: another reason to stay away from them. Once back on the boat we made a mad dash here. We over shot our mark."

"Glad you made it out of both situations. Hope the boat is okay. We do boat repair, if you need anything."

"Good to know. Got to talk over some things with my friends." He turned away.

Tom was about to leave when a lady approached him. "Hi. My name is Hope Mayo. I'm a friend of Alberta Parsons."

"My counselor?" Tom asked.

"Yes. She has told me a bit about your dreams. No, I won't tell anyone, this was in strictest confidence. She only shared because I'm a believer in dreams also. But I have a big problem and I thought you might be able to dream for me."

Tom laughed, "It doesn't work that way. The dreams just come to me and tell me the future, sometimes."

"Before going to bed tonight, please ask if I'll soon be getting a retirement package from Kodak. They are giving these packages to only a few people. I want to know if I'll be getting one."

"I wish I could help you but I've never heard of that before. I'm sure that I don't have that ability."

"I think you do. I'll be talking to you tomorrow since we'll be spending the night on our boat. Who knows when this fog will clear."

"See you tomorrow then." Tom turned to see if he could catch the conversation around Seaman Gary but they had drifted outside to sit on a picnic table.

He stopped BJ and asked if he'd talked to Gary.

"I had a hard time trying to start a conversation with him. It's curious they were checking out Devil's Nose, in a sailboat. If it were official business, he'd be on the Cutter or some other Coast Guard boat. His buddies would all be seaman."

"That's what I thought." Tom replied. "That lady over there just asked me to dream for her."

BJ laughed. "Never heard of such a thing."

"That's what I told her. Isn't Mrs. Parsons supposed to keep our conversations private?"

"You'd think so. Just let it go. No big deal."

"What if she told Seaman Gary or someone he knows?"

"I doubt they travel in the same circles. Don't worry about it. If this lady approaches you again, I'll be right there to make sure dreams are not mentioned."

*****

Tom crawled into his bed up at the big house. The fog still lay heavy on everything and everything on the Playhouse would be damp.

Everyone had gotten a ride home except the couple tied up to Candy Kiss. They had a portable heater and said they'd be just fine. Gary and his pals would be back the next day to help get their sailboat off the rocky beach.

It was a busy day. Tom was tired and forgot all about Mrs. Mayo's request for a dream. But the giver of dreams did not forget. Tom closed his eyes to hear the roar of roller skates on a wooden floor. Then he saw Mrs. Mayo whirling around a corner on skates with a big grin and a sign that said 'retired.'

Tom shot up and wrote it down. What was that about, he wondered. Power of suggestion? He wanted to learn more about the Nazi but he fell into a sound sleep. No dreams that night.

CHAPTER SEVEN

Cary was shaking Tom awake.

"What are you doing here?" he asked as he gathered his blankets around him.

Cary grabbed his pillow away and shouted again, "Get Up! Cindy sent me up. She's got breakfast going in the yacht club building."

"So early?" Tom looked at the clock as he made a grab for the pillow and missed. It was after eight. "Oh, so sorry. Am I in trouble?"

"No, Mrs. Mayo wants to see you before she leaves - and the crew from the beached sailboat are here. BJ needs your help with the dragline. Can you drive it close enough on the beach to pick up the sailboat?"

"I think so. If our straps are long enough. But I'm sure BJ will be driving it, not me." Suddenly they heard the load roaring sound of the machine starting up. BJ would be driving the dragline on the road that took them from the back of the property where they had been digging a new channel for more docks last winter.

They'd had the machine up front this spring where BJ had driven it onto a barge to remove the plant growth and rocks that had washed into the channel over the winter. Now it was in the back to launch bigger boats and just to keep it out of sight.

"Leave, I've got to get up! Wait in the hall! It'll take a while for him to get that beast up front." Cindy left.

She talked through the now closed door. "The crew of the boat brought some long straps with them."

"I might have to go into the water to put the straps around the boat. Good to know. It'll be cold. Grab some extra towels out of the bathroom, please. I have a feeling someone will need them and it might be me." Tom said. "I need to show my face so BJ knows I'm coming but tell Cindy that I want some of that breakfast. I don't know what to tell Mrs. Mayo, but I'll be right down."

Cary left and Tom got washed and dressed in record time. He picked up his note about the dream to take to Mrs, Mayo, hoping no words would have to be spoken about his dream as to whether it was a true prediction or not.

As Tom watched from the club house, the drag-line made its slow approach to the beach. Tom started to laugh. Cindy wanted to know what was so funny about going under that big sailboat.

"It's not that," Tom answered. "I was just remembering last winter and BJ walking around out there in his brown Carhartt outfit.

Cindy laughed also. "I know what you're thinking."

"What's so funny?" Mr. Mayo asked.

Cindy explained. "BJ has a one-piece suit of Carharts that he wears to work outside in the winter. It's actually called a duck suit. He's covered in a warm one-piece outfit, with boots to the top of his head. You tell it, Tom."

"One sunny day when the snow covered the ground and we were getting breakfast up at the house, we looked out the window. We could see almost the whole marina from our kitchen window. We saw BJ walking around in his brown outfit with a huge brown duck, looked to be the same exact color, following him around."

"We looked it up and it had to be a Muscovy duck. They're the largest duck and not native to this area." Cindy added.

"He was off his path, that's for sure." Tom couldn't stop laughing so Cindy took over.

"He must have thought BJ was a relative, or a girlfriend. They were exactly the same color; the duck came up to BJ's waist. BJ just kept walking around like he didn't know the duck was behind him, but he did. We wondered if it was mating season, what BJ would do. What a time to not have a camera handy!"

That brought a laugh to all of them. It was time to go out to the lake and see what BJ had in mind as far as getting that boat unstuck from the bottom. It had been there all night and it was still in the same place. That was lucky.

The crew of the sailboat hooked up the straps to make a sling, attached it to the bucket of the tall drag-line. Tom took the sling end and made his way through the water to the sailboat. It was not going to work - too short. BJ lowered the bucket and the straps were taken off. Next idea!

Jerry, the skipper of a 30 foot Penn Yan boat with a tunnel drive stood nearby and offered his boat to (hopefully) pull the sailboat off the beach. His boat had the out-drive and propeller tucked in a tunnel up under the boat and could go in much more shallow water than most boats that had their motors hanging low in the water. He ran to his boat saying to Tom, "Meet me in the water; I'm taking Cary with me to handle the ropes and boat if I'm needed aft!"

Cary jumped up and ran after him.

As Jerry's boat pulled close to the back end of the sailboat, Tom waded up to the swim platform. Cary handed him a coil of ropes. Tom then swam to the sailboat. After jumping a few times, he found a place to hook the ropes. He threaded a good sized loop from one aft cleat to another then got safely out of the way to see what would happen.

"Cary!"Jerry yelled. "Lie down on the deck, close to the motor block, in case the cleats break loose and the rope comes flying back at us!"

Cary lay flat on the floor behind the big motor box in the center, aft of Jerry's boat. The motor revved, the boat moved, and Cary heard cheering from the beach. They'd done it!

Tom climbed aboard Jerry's swim platform and guided the sailboat into the harbor alongside the channel wall. The sailboat's crew jumped on board, let the ropes loose, thanked everyone and took off.

"What a let down." Tom said. "They didn't even wait to let us haul the boat out of the water and see what damage had been done."

Next, the Mayos' boat pulled out of the harbor, Mr. and Mrs. waved goodbye to everyone. BJ started up the beast and made his way to the back of the property. Jerry, Cary, Cindy and Tom went back to finish breakfast in the clubhouse. Cary took Tom aside.

"What was in that note you slipped to Mrs. Mayo?"

"Someone told her about my dreams. She wanted me to dream for her. Ask God if she was going to get a retirement offer from Kodak soon."

"I don't believe it! It doesn't work that way, number one. Number two, who told her about your dreams?"

"She admitted my counselor was a friend of hers."

"Did you have a dream for her?"

"I don't know. She was in the dream I had. Wouldn't it be cool if it worked that way? Keep this between us."

"I will. But she can't be talking about what's said in your sessions."

"I agree! I called her right away yesterday and told her so. She was so nice and very apologetic. We'll just wait and see where this goes. I worry about my Devil's Nose dream. I feel that someone is talking about that. I've had two, maybe three different people warn me away from diving there."

"Can I come with you when you do?" She knew him well.

"After the last warning, BJ says he's going to be my dive partner. You can handle the boat while we're down there."

"When are you planning on going?"

"Not sure we can plan it. Things keep happening, like this fog yesterday and the sailboat that needed hauling off the beach, but soon, I hope." Tom replied. "I need to get down to Braddock's Bay marina the rest of today. We'll get there way before that sailboat does. It docks there, I found out. We'll probably hoist it out of the water there to see what damage was done. I'd like to see the marks on the keel from being stuck in the rocks at the base of Devil's Nose."

CHAPTER EIGHT

BJ and Tom, being able to travel a couple of hours faster than a sailboat, stopped at the POW camp. There were more people walking the path around the perimeter, which was leveled and graveled to make the walking easier. They even saw an elderly man on a motorized scooter going from sign to sign. Each sign held a note about which barracks, community building, offices and store were situated on that spot, plus a photo of the inside of the building.

"Pretty fancy and comfortable for a prisoner of war camp," remarked Tom.

"It wasn't always a prisoner of war camp. It started out as a CCC camp back in 1935. President Roosevelt set up what he called a conservation corps to provide jobs and money for able adults. They came in, it's here on this sign, and actually built this park. They built the roads, bike paths, and took down trees for the large parking lots and access to the beach."

"They did a good job! It's beautiful here, my favorite park, although I can't say I've seen many parks." BJ laughed.

"You have many years ahead of you to see the country, once you finish college." BJ wasn't going to let that go. Tom decided to play along as long as it made BJ feel better about selling his mother's house.

As the old saying goes, time goes by fast when you're having fun. BJ looked at his watch and yelped. "We've got to get going. That sailboat just might be there by now!" They raced to BJ's pickup and then went as fast as they dared to Braddock's Bay marina.

As they drove in they saw a crowd around the boat hauler, the now infamous sailboat high in its slings. Out of the pick-up, they made their way through the crowd to discover Seaman Gary and Sam Sanders in a heated argument.

"They'll be here any minute." Sam was saying. "You should have waited for them!"

"I know what I'm doing and you might say that I'm their boss. I got them this job!"

"Hold on a minute," BJ spoke up. "Where did you get the key for the machine? Tell me later!" He was looking at the sailboat hanging in the slings of the huge boat hauler.

Turning to the crowd, BJ continued "Nothing to see here, folks. We'll be in the office in a few minutes, if you need us." The crowd disbursed.

Tom was looking at the keel which had deep gouges along the top of the keel where it had evidently slid between two table rocks hidden in the water at the base of Devil's Nose.

"Lucky it didn't break off."

BJ turned to Tom, "Tom, you go talk to Sam, I'll talk to Gary."

Tom turned and made a dash to Sam's boat. He'd already gotten on board. "Permission to come aboard, sir!" Sam gave him a big smile and came back out to the rail.

"I didn't know that guy was with the Coast Guard and he'd had your permission to haul his boat. I was just looking out for your best interests, like I said I would."

"You did good. We stopped along the way, lost track of time but he moved a lot faster than we thought he would. Sorry we weren't here. Thanks for trying to cover for us. Actually, we thought Coast Guard personnel were still here."

"They were until that guy showed up. That's how I found out that he was Coast Guard. He told them to go back to the station and he'd cover for them until you got here. I just didn't feel right even though. Then he wanted to argue. Guess he picked the wrong guy. Sorry for that!"

"He's had a couple of bad days. Got his boat stuck in the table rocks at the base of Devil's Nose. They were able to stand on the rocks and push his boat out. Then the fog rolled in and he lost track of where he was. He then washed up on our beach. He had to find a ride to Rochester and back this morning, and we had quite a time getting him off the shore this morning! All the time, I imagine, he was worried about his keel. All is safe now. I'll see you later."

Tom raced back to talk to BJ to see the damage and what they were going to do about it. Instead, he saw someone in the office waving to him.

Pretty little Leanne from the boat 'Get Away' was waiting for him. "I don't know what he told you but I heard Seaman Gary's side. He didn't tell the whole truth. I've no idea what it all means but the argument wasn't about using the hauler. It was more about Gary going diving at Devil's Nose without him. Sam wanted to know how long this had been going on. He thought they had an arrangement. I don't trust people who lie and I thought you should know. I thought it might make sense to you."

"Thanks Leanne, It sort of makes sense but why lie? And why those two working together? Thanks."

Tom went out to hear what Gary was saying to BJ. Leanne went back to the 'Get Away'.

"I have the name of a guy who does fiberglass work in the office. If you don't have anyone, I'll call him to stop over."

"That'd be great. Can we leave it in the slings until he's finished?"

"Give it a try. If no other large boats come to get hauled, which I doubt. You'll be all right overnight, or for a few days, at the most.

This guy lives nearby - I'll stress the importance of fixing it right away. We should clear up the space in the slings, for sure. But don't worry. Tom has used these slings many times. He's very good at it," BJ told Gary.

BJ met Tom halfway and told him Sam was trying to manage the marina and Gary objected. So, Sam got a little hot under the collar. Gary, being tired, gave him hot words right back. It was good we got here when we did. We might have had a fight on our hands.

"Leanne from the boat 'Get Away' told me a different story." Tom proceeded to tell BJ what Leanne had said.

"This gets weirder by the day. Gary and Sam working together? It must be big!"

"Or they think it is. To me, you'd have to be able to carry whatever it is in a Nazi helmet. Oh yeah. I didn't tell you about my dream last night. We were having a big birthday party for Cary- live music and her whole school was there. Even the Nazi showed up."

"When is her birthday?"

"I don't remember."

"Another wait and see. Mrs. Parsons heard this one yet?"

No, not yet."

"Maybe it's marking the day we find the helmet, a cause for a celebration."

"I'll be glad when this is over."

"We'll dive sometime this week. Got to get it in before your second class begins. Well, we know Gary works on Thursday; why not plan it then? I hope it doesn't take more than one dive!"

"Sounds like a plan. Now to get Judge Travers on board and the weather cooperating."

*****

Judge Travers had just finished putting gas in a boat and was writing up the sales slip when BJ drove in. "All is quiet here, Boss," the judge quipped.

"Don't tell me you heard about the ruckus at Braddock's Bay." BJ asked.

"Then I won't tell you. Did you have trouble?"

"We got there late and Gary had already hauled his boat. One story was that Sam Sanders tried to stop him. They were in a big argument when we pulled in."

"The other story?"

"A nearby person understood that Sam was angry at Gary for going diving at Devil's Nose without him. It's wasn't their deal."

"Wow, that puts a different spin on things. What does the mafia want with any findings at the Nose? They must think it's big. Anything of historical importance belongs to the state."

"Not if they take it out of state, or out of the country, even. They could get away with it. It must gall them to think that Tom knows something. I'd better keep an eye on him. How would they know he even knows anything?"

"Has he shared his dream with anyone besides you, Cindy, me and Mrs. Parsons?" The judge asked.

"Mrs. Parsons sent a friend to Tom for an answer to a problem she had, but I doubt she shared any particular dream. She's already apologized and knows that was against her rules."

"That reminds me. I'll give Tom a call. Some lady called him about a dream. She said Tom would understand. She is Mrs. Mayo and was here this week when the fog rolled in." The judge took out his phone and dialed Tom.

"Tom, Judge Travers here. You had a call from Mrs. Mayo. She said to tell you that she got a retirement package today from Kodak." There was a long pause at Tom's end.

"Tom......, she said you would understand and to thank you."

"Yeah, yeah, thanks Judge, I sort of understand - but I didn't do anything." Tom laughed, "Does she think that I have a magical pull at Kodak? Thanks for telling me."

"One more thing now that I have you and BJ together." He put the phone on speaker. "Cary has a birthday coming up soon and we'd like to surprise her with a big splash here at the marina. Say, in two weeks, Saturday night? I'd like to get a band and invite her classmates. A secret, of course, if we can."

BJ spoke first. "Sure Judge, can't say no to you with all your family does to help us. It'll be a lot of fun, hard to keep a secret but we'll do our best."

Tom chimed in, "That sounds great. Maybe I can ask her out, to the movies or something. Then I'll get sick and have to come back early."

"Tom, I wonder about your devious mind, but I'll offer to drive you."

BJ spoke up. "Or Cindy and I can make it a double date and the judge can stay here and greet everyone. Cindy's good at playing sick. Remember last year when you all surprised me with the family reunion?"

"Oh, yeah. That was great fun. We need to do that again." Tom replied. "Judge, ask BJ if I can spend the night here."

"BJ's shaking his head no. I'd like to see that operation. How about I come to pick you up about eight? I'll bring the girls."

"Fine with me," Tom replied.

CHAPTER NINE

"Tom, let's do a little investigating about this Devil's Nose thing."

"We're going diving tomorrow, right?"

"Yes. I'm thinking it might be good to hike up to that point on Devil's Nose where you saw the soldier. It might help our dive if you can tell us exactly which direction he threw his helmet... before we dive."

"Oh, I got you. Seaman Gary's already been looking and evidently not finding anything. The dream might help us find it. Good thinking. But, the soldier is also at the party, so I was told in my second dream."

"Cindy," BJ said. "Tom and I are going to the top of the Nose and do a little looking around. Keep that to yourself, but can you and the girls take care of the marina while we stop off there on our way to Braddock's?"

"No problem. You might loose your job here, though. We have everything so well under control. Who needs men?" She laughed and so did Cary and Nina, overhearing that last as they walked up to join the conversation.

Nina spoke up for once. "This marina's never looked so good."

Then they all laughed. Nina was new to this country and this marina. "You're learning English too good," Tom said.

"Not too good, too well," Nina countered.

"I give up," Tom said.

"Don't even start with women," BJ laughingly told him as he climbed in the pick-up truck. Tom hurried around and got into the other side.

"Here's a couple of sandwiches and a soda if you get hungry," Cindy handed him a small cooler.

"Thanks, Mom," Tom joked.

"By the way," Cindy continued. "We did a lot of organizing at your Gram's house. Maybe you should find some time to go over and pick out anything important to you before the yard sale."

"Oh, great!" Tom replied. "That's important, too. BJ? Can we find time for that?"

"Soon." BJ replied. "You got everything organized already?"

"Well, we know what we want to do, but you need to say if there is anything of your mother's that you want to bring home. We got all the diaries for Tom." Cindy replied.

"That's great! Maybe some evening, before dark. Did you see any signs of other people being there?"

"Yes, we set those things aside and notified the sheriff. He wants you to look it over before we file a report. He'll send a regular patrol by there and see if anyone comes back. A couple of things are odd and might hold clues."

"We'll stop by tonight."

"The things I thought didn't belong there are the ones on the dining room table. I could be wrong, so you'd best look at it before I call the sheriff back."

"Thanks, we'll get over there later for sure."

*****

Tom huffed to the top of Devil's Nose on their way to try to figure out his Nazi dream. "What a view!" he said. Then turning back to the path. "Come on old man!"

BJ came to the top a few feet after Tom. "Watch what you say. I was right behind you all the way until I tripped on that limb you put in my path."

"Don't blame me for Mother Nature! Like I said," he waved his arms out toward the lake! "look at that view!"

"Wow! I should have done this a long time ago. Can you figure out where you were in your dream?"

"Well, there's more than one big tree up here. It was a huge chestnut tree. Don't know how I knew that, I can't tell one tree from another. Let me try standing behind a couple, see if it feels right. Oh, look. Chestnuts on the ground! This must be the one. And look, there's a big rock over there."

Tom moved around until he found the position behind the tree that gave him the view he had in the dream.

"Where was the soldier standing when he threw 'whatever' into the lake?"

Tom moved behind the rock, stood up, took a few steps like a pitcher winding up on the pitcher's mound, and threw an imaginary helmet into the lake. Just like he saw in his dream.

"It went off to the west of the Nose! Not into the table rocks at all!" Tom exclaimed. "If it's there, coming directly to the Nose in a boat would be coming from the wrong direction. It should be in this little bay. It was a long time ago. Wouldn't the currents, waves and storms have moved it?"

"Not necessarily. It could only go as far as the rocks. It might be wedged up against the rocks on that side. If it went the other way, it would have washed up on the beach. Likely, someone would have found it. Well, let's get going. Now, we have a place to dive tomorrow. If we don't find it, let's hope it's either on that private beach or someone has it on a shelf in their living room."

They hiked down the path to their pick-up and made a mad dash for Braddock's and Tom's other job. "Don't tell anyone what we're thinking or doing."

Tom hopped out at Braddock's and BJ turned around to get back to his own marina.

*****

It was hard to keep his mouth closed about their discovery. Soon he noticed a couple of boats waiting at the gas dock for him. He pumped their gas and then went back into the office and tacked the map of the docking system to a wall.

Keep busy, he told himself. That's the best way to keep my mouth shut.

Some new people came to see if any docks were available, just in time to show off his map. During the afternoon, he took in three new customers and added their names to the map.

The judge and the two girls drove into the parking lot to take Tom home. Tom was busy with new customers and never even touched the sandwiches Cindy had packed for him. They'd keep all night in the refrigerator.

One of the new customers knew the Judge and they got to talking. The judge convinced them to come out to BJ's marina instead of docking at Braddock's Bay. When he told Tom, Tom wondered if that would be okay with the county. The Judge said a person had a right to go where he wanted. "I'm not pulling anyone away from Braddock's. Absolutely not!" Tom said.

*****

BJ and Tom made a quick stop at Gram's house. Amazingly, it was sort of clean. Those women had worked wonders. Stepping into the dining room, they found some strange things on the table, an underwater metal detector, a computer, flippers and snorkel, and cigar wrappers.

BJ pulled out his phone and called Cindy. She answered on the first ring.

"Hi!"

"Okay, I'm calling the sheriff. Think he'll be in?"

"Yes. It's his home phone number I gave you. Not much exciting happens in his life. I think he'll be right over."

"He should move in with us if he wants excitement. We might be a little while. See you as soon as we can. Bye."

BJ hung up and called the number Cindy had given him for Sheriff Green.

"Hi Sheriff, This is BJ of BJ's Marina. You spoke to my wife earlier. I'm at my mother's house on County Line Rd. We have definitely been broken into."

"The house has been empty for some time and there are some items here that don't belong to us. The things they left suspiciously tie into another thing we've been investigating. Do you think you might pick them up and see if you can get any information off them, fingerprints or what they were looking at on a computer?"

"I'm just down the road from you. I'll be right over. Don't touch them, if you haven't already."

"No, we haven't touched them. Don't know about my wife."

"She assured me that she moved them with a small cloth. They were already on the table."

"Still there." BJ replied. "See you in a few minutes."

"I hope The sheriff's not a member of the mafia." Tom said.

BJ laughed. "We can't get that unlucky two years in a row. I hear he ran a stiff race when the other sheriff died. He's got to know all about that. He'd better be straight."

BJ called Cindy back. "Hon, the sheriff is on his way. Shouldn't take long. You didn't touch them, did you?"

"No, they were sitting right on the table where you found them. We didn't even clean the floor around the table. Remember, I had the Judge's wife with me. We walked into that room and both said 'Oh-oh.' It put a halt to our cleaning."

"The kitchen and living room look ready to show. Thanks. You got a bonus coming for that."

"Tom told us about wanting her diaries, so we got them first. They're all in this house now. Don't take too much time looking around. You haven't spent much time at home."

"We'll stay up and talk tonight. I can come back here another night. Maybe you'll come with us."

"That'll be helpful."

"I hear tires in the driveway. Talk to you in a little while. Bye Babe!"

"Bye!"

CHAPTER TEN

Back at BJ's Marina, Tom, BJ and Cindy stayed up late, talking about that thing (they weren't supposed to talk about) with Cindy - the birthday party. They were excited but about midnight the marine radio slammed out a call. No proper use of the call signs, just "Help! Help! I've run aground. I need help!" BJ grabbed the mic. "What's your name, skipper?" He was trying to get him to calm down. The answer he got was "Help!"

"Skipper," BJ said. "Where were you coming from?"

"I don't know, it's all dark out here, I ran up on a beach or something."

"Can you switch to channel 18?"

The skipper switched. Tom reached over and covered the mic, "He's at Devil's Nose. That's why he's so loud."

BJ nodded yes and spoke into the mic. "We're close by and can be there in about twenty minutes or less. Stay calm. How many people on board?"

"There are four of us, Two adults and two teenagers."

"I'll turn the mic over to my wife, Cindy. She'll keep talking to you until we get our boat going. Don't worry, we're on our way. This is BJ of BJ's marina."

He and Tom ran for warmer clothing and grabbed some for the people, too. They got the Dutch Tug revved up and out of the channel in record time. Sure enough, there was a boat plowed into the beach on the west side of Devil's Nose. They carefully backed up as close as they dared get to the beach, threw an anchor, and helped the people wade into the water to board the Dutch Tug's swim platform into BJ's boat. Those dry clothes came in handy! Everyone was shivering from wading in the cold water.

The skipper wanted them to haul his boat off the beach right then but seeing as how the adults reeked of alcohol, BJ gave an adamant no. There was room for them to stay in BJ's house and they could go back out first thing in the morning. Better to haul in the daylight. "Less damage was likely to be done to the boat," they told the skipper. They attached some extra anchors to the boat so it wouldn't go anywhere.

The skipper kept saying he was sorry, over and over again. Tom and BJ shared a look that said something about this being where they planned on diving tomorrow anyway. Why not do it under the guise of saving a boat. Tom, driving, they made for BJ's marina.

*****

Cindy rang the little kitchen bell she kept to let BJ and Tom know breakfast was ready. She'd given them an extra hour due to the late hour they all got to bed. She choked down a laugh at the condition of the boat's crew as they paraded up from the basement, the kids still in makeshift pajamas. The gentleman. in borrowed clothes, sat at the table and kept his head in his hands.

"Would you like a couple of aspirin?" she asked. He nodded yes. Then noticing the condition of the others, she decided to bring the bottle of pills. "You must be on vacation, with all the celebrating."

One of the teenagers answered, saying it was her brother's twenty-first birthday. Teaching them about drinking was a rite of passage, according to her father. She added that she'd pass next year when it was her turn. She'd rather have a new hair-do, and a sexy dress. Her head was also resting on her hands.

"Sounds like either way could lead to trouble," Cindy added, a slight smile on her face in case anyone looked up to catch her laughing at them. Just then BJ and Tom came in from outside. Cindy gave them a big smile, just short of a laugh.

"The girls are here, ready to work. Can you handle things here if I take them with us?" BJ asked Cindy, gathering his plate and food from the skillet on the stove. Tom followed suit.

"Sure," replied Cindy.

Turning to their guests, BJ asked, "You guys almost ready to go save your boat?" That brought groans from the occupants of the table.

"Tell you what, all we need is the skipper. The rest of you can take it slow. It might take a couple of hours. Go back to sleep. When we get it back here, we should take a look at the bottom, that'll take a little more time. Okay with you, skipper?"

"I'm good to go." He rose, staggering a bit and sat down again.

"Okay, I've got to have a word with my helpers. Someone will come get you when we're ready - or you can just wander down, but give me a few minutes for a meeting with my employees."

"Okay," groaned the skipper once more.

Tom and BJ wolfed down their breakfasts and hurried out the door. Cary and Nina were right outside. They headed down to the marina office and inside before a word was said.

"You both know about Tom's dream of the Nazi throwing his helmet from the top of Devil's Nose." They both nodded yes.

"Yesterday, Tom and I hiked to the top of the Nose to see if we could get an idea of which direction he threw in whatever he threw. We got a good idea it went in the water right where that boat ran ashore. The water is very shallow there. We'll all get into the water, saying we want to take a look at any damage that might be done, and we'll be hooking up the ropes. We'll put the skipper in the boat first so he has no idea what we're really doing."

Tom took over. "While you're being ever so helpful, checking out the boat and attaching the ropes, shuffle you feet. See if you can find anything unusual in the water there. Maybe find some pretty stones you hand to him to take back as a souvenir. Anything really good or unusual, put in your pockets. We'll leave you on the beach to hike back, being such a nice day. Don't let anyone see you looking for treasure. The mafia is looking for this also, and you don't want to get in their arrow sites."

Cary laughed, "I think that phrase you're looking for is cross-hairs, Tom."

Nina laughed, "I knew that. It was on TV last night."

Tom gave her a hard look. "Wish I could learn Spanish that quick! You sure you didn't know it before you got here?"

"I picked up a little at the farm, working in the fields, but mostly from the Travers family and TV. You move to Mexico and see how fast you pick up the language," Nina said.

BJ, in a great mood, expecting to find a treasure today, joked, "My luck, I'd get to Mexico and they'd all speak English! Okay, go see if you can get this skipper moving. I'll gas up the Dutch Tug and move it up by the house."

Tom and the girls ran up to the house to get the skipper.

They met him just coming out of the house.

CHAPTER ELEVEN

They all piled in the Tug. The skipper of the other boat was looking a little better. They drove out the channel and took a wide right turn, cruising along the beach towards Devil's Nose. They soon could make out the beached twenty four foot boat. As they got closer, they realized the motor was nowhere in sight and there was a hole in the transom where the motor used to be

"Do you imagine someone stripped the boat?" asked the skipper.

"It's so early in the morning, and no-one's around. Let's not panic until we get there and know for sure," BJ said. "Wow, look at your transom! It's got a big hole ripped in it."

"I'd better go real carefully," Tom suggested. "The motor might be below in the water somewhere." BJ agreed.

"You did a good job, Skipper," BJ tried to joke.

"Maybe we should just leave my boat here," suggested the skipper. He groaned, "I just took out a big loan on it."

"Don't give up yet," BJ said. "I know a guy who has fixed worse than that. We need to get the motor out of the water though and work on that. You do have insurance on it, don't you?"

"Yeah, I got insurance but do they insure when it's my own stupidity?"

"We'll work with the insurance. Which company do you have?" The skipper told him. "We work with them all the time. Shouldn't be any problem."

Tom threw out the anchor and they all climbed out in about three feet of water. BJ directed the skipper to climb in the boat while they searched the water for parts.

Cary soon yelled out, "I got the motor, don't know why I can't lift it." This brought a laugh from all of them, seeing as how it likely weighed about four hundred pounds.

"Maybe we need to come back with the barge and some lifting equipment."

"It's in more than one piece."

"Pick up what you can. Tom will be there to help you mark it so nothing else runs over it."

They saw Cary stick something in her pocket. Tom got there, tied a balloon to the motor and proceeded to search the bottom, supposedly for pieces of the motor. He picked up something and took a quick look at what Cary had put in her pocket.

BJ was fixing the ropes. Nina was surveying the bottom of the boat, all the while glancing in different directions to see what she could see.

Tom yelled, "We got the propeller!"

Nina glanced up and met BJ's eyes. She nodded her head, she found something also.

"On second thought," BJ called, "tie a rope around it. Between the five of us, maybe we can pull it onto the beach. Then we leave the girls to guard it. I'll get permission to drive our pickup on the beach and we can take it home and get right to work on it."

They put a rope round what was left of the motor, and the five of them took up positions along the rope to try to pull it in closer to the beach. The buoyancy of the water helped, once they got it to move. Their momentum brought it halfway onto the beach. It wasn't going any further. They attached an anchor around it and also to the bushes on the beach so it wouldn't float back out. It was out of the path for towing the boat off the beach and out into the water and home.

With ropes attached to the beached boat, BJ climbed back into the Tug. The skipper of his boat was behind that wheel; everyone else got far away. The towing began. The boat moved swiftly off the beach. The skipper transferred the ropes to the bow so BJ could tow it from the front.

Towing from the back with the hole in the transom was like scooping up the water. They had to tow from the front. Tom jumped in the sick boat and began bailing out the water that had already come in. The hole in the aft was quite big. Their friend, Chad, would love to get his hands on this repair. Tom could see the before and after pictures he'd put on Facebook already.

As they gently pulled away from the shore and toward BJ's Marina, the girls could be seen going back into the water to search some more. Maybe they'd find some special stones for a keepsake of this adventure for the skipper.

CHAPTER TWELVE

They pulled the injured boat up to the gas dock and were met by Judge Travers.

"Where are the girls?" he asked.

"We left them on the beach to guard the motor. As soon as I get this on a trailer, I'll go get them in the truck so we can bring the motor back, too."

Tom ran to hook an empty trailer to the pickup. He got in and backed it down the launch ramp and soon had the boat safe on dry ground.

"And that boy is worried about getting his driver's license?" the Judge asked of no one in particular.

"Tom, Skipper, jump in the back and we'll go get the girls and the motor."

"I'll be waiting here. Don't need my muscle," joked the Judge.

The skipper's wife came running, "Can we leave when you get done? My brother is here to take us to our car."

"Sure, I guess," replied the skipper.

"Go ahead now, we'll manage the motor. We have this handy crank on the truck for just this kind of thing. Leave your phone number and name with my wife."

The skipper jumped out.

"Thanks for everything! Call me when you have an idea of what you have to do and how long it'll take. Also how much it will cost me."

"Sure thing. Stay safe." BJ headed out the drive to Troutberg, the little community that lay between the marina and Devil's Nose. He was sending up silent prayers that the driveway closest to the Nose was available so he could drive onto the beach.

*****

They were in luck. Nobody was parked anywhere near the last house. BJ had a feeling it had been empty for a while. The driveway ended directly on the beach. It was a short distance to where the girls were standing with a Coast Guard boat anchored not far away. Seaman Gary was standing next to them. Tom and BJ's hearts were nearly stopped! What was he doing there? They wondered.

Tom jumped out and guided the pickup now going backwards on the rocky beach. "Fancy meeting you here," shouted BJ.

"We saw the girls on the beach, recognized Cary from other times I've seen her at the marina, and decided to stop and chat."

"Great!" replied BJ. Tom wondered if BJ'd lost his mind.

"Maybe you can help Tom and I hoist this motor in the truck instead of the girls."

"What have you got in your pockets?" BJ winked at the girls.

"We found some neat polished glass stones and some other nice ones that might make a nice remembrance for the family," Cary answered.

"I've got some for myself," smiled Nina. "

"Get in the cab of the truck and we'll have this baby hoisted in no time. Gary, thanks for stopping by. You should have seen this drunken party last night about midnight."

"They heard the transmission in Rochester but knew you were right there and able. I have to thank you. So they were drunk?"

"Yes, a family, two adults and two teenagers. Sad mess. Drove right up on the beach. Said they couldn't see in the dark. They'll pay for the repairs! I'll get to make some money for a change!"

"If they object to the price, let them know how lucky they are that you came to their rescue - and not me! They'd have gotten a ticket or worse! Life's lessons can be hard," replied Gary. "Well, you have her under control. Hey, she's missing a propeller."

"That's inside the boat at my place. You're welcome to stop by and see it."

"We just might do that."Gary got in his dingy and rowed back out to the Coast Guard Cutter44. Tom, BJ and the girls watched them turn around and head for BJ's Marina.

Tom turned to the girls. "Did you find anything?"

"Yes, we found a helmet. We hid it in the bushes, just in time so Gary didn't see it! Here it is!" She pulled a water-logged old helmet out of the bushes.

"We have what the soldier showed me in my dream. Now, what to do with it?" asked Tom.

"Let's just keep it between us, Cindy, and the Judge for now. We'll wait and see if Tom gets some direction from his dreams."

"No! Wait!" declared Nina. "I have something that might be dog tags." She held up a long rope of a thing, encrusted with seaweed.

"I think we've got the whole thing. Maybe the Nazi will come back into my life one more time and tell me what to do with them. Let's just hold onto them. Maybe we'll clean them up and wait a couple of weeks to see if anything else happens. I'd like to know why Gary and Sam are looking for them, also." BJ nodded yes. The girls looked at each other, puzzled, but okay with Tom's decision. It was his dream and meant nothing to them.

"Let's get back to the marina."

When they drove in, the 44Cutter was already parked at the gas dock and the crew was making a beeline to the broken boat. Its name, in the back, looked like Lucky Lady, but some letters were missing.

Gary saw BJ pull in and shouted, "That doesn't look like a Lucky Lady to me!"

They crowded around, oowing and awing over all the damage. Tom had quickly transferred the treasures into the Judge's car.

No safer place, he thought. The judge spoke up, "If Tom is ready, I'll take him to Braddock's Bay. Don't want to be too late for work there."

Seaman Gary turned to say, "I think I heard the bosses interviewing someone who can afford to branch out and run another marina. That should be a relief for you."

"Oh, good!" Tom said. "When do you think we'll officially hear? I like it there but word's getting around about BJ's mechanic skills - I'll be needed more here. We can't always rely on a retired judge to be in charge here. We caught him sleeping on the job one day."

The judge moved in to pinch Tom's arm while the others giggled. Tom didn't dare to fight back. "We love you, Judge!" he shouted, instead.

"We've got to get going," Gary announced. "Stay away from those rocks at Devil's Nose," he told Tom. "You guys were lucky this morning."

BJ spoke up. "We've been there enough times, rescuing boaters - we have no desire to get into trouble ourselves."

Gary's crew had the Cutter turned around and waited for him to join them. They headed out to the lake and BJ and Tom gave a sigh of relief. "I thought they'd never leave," Tom said.

"What's this smelly stuff you sneaked into my car?" Judge Travers asked.

"I think we have what the Nazi threw into the lake," Tom replied.

"Let's take it up to Cindy, and see if she can clean it up."

"Carefully," said Tom.

"She'll be careful. But I need to get you off to Braddock's Bay."

"I'll take him," the Judge said. "I don't want to be caught sleeping again."

Just joking," said Tom. "You can take a nap any time you want, so long as we know where to find you. If BJ stays here, he can take a better look at Gram's house to see if there's anything he wants to move in here."

"That's exactly what I'll do, besides helping with the clean-up there and here. Maybe those dogtags have a name still visible on them, or a number someone can trace."

"Maybe he is a long-lost relative of ours," Tom said. "That reminds me." He turned to the girls.

"In your spare time, would you read Gram's diaries and tell me about them later? I'm most interested in the time around 1944, when the POW Camp opened. We might find a clue as to the identity of that German soldier. I'd like to know why he's coming to me in my dreams."

"Well, Tom's given us all our orders for the day," Judge said. "Let's get going." This brought a big laugh from them all as they disbursed in different directions.

BJ took the treasures from the backseat on the floor of the Judge's car. He headed up to the house. The girls followed him to get some of the diaries to read. Tom got in the Judge's car and they set out on the Lake Ontario State Parkway to Braddock's Bay Marina.

CHAPTER THIRTEEN

Cary and Nina retrieved some of the diaries they'd promised to read from the big house. They walked down to the clubhouse, where the furniture was more comfortable, then turned a couple of chairs around so they could watch the gas dock and launch ramp and settled in to read.

"Cary, this in an English I no read!" Nina said.

"It is oldfashioned wording and it looks like she might have been lying down. See how sometimes a line of script runs close to the one above it?" Cary leaned over, pointing out the sentence she was talking about.

"I'm not going to be any help if I no understand it," Nina said.

"I've got an idea. Get a pad of paper and a pen and when I find something interesting, I'll read it to you. You can make a short note, and write down the page I'm on, so Tom can go to any important parts of the diary right away."

"Okay. I'll look in the office for pen and paper. I may have to run up to the house."

"Okay. This is already interesting."

"What date did you pick up?

"I started with Jan of 1950. Run!"

Nina ended up at the house to see if they had a pad of paper she could have. Cindy had just put the helmet and tags into some warm sudsy water to soak the sludge away. Then the items were going over to Gram's house.

Nina came running back with a clean pad of paper. "Anything good?"

"Not really what we're looking for. Life was sure different then. Gram had a date with her boyfriend James. It was winter then and they didn't have the clothes we have now, nor the heat. They had one central woodburning stove. Gram's parents were in the living room by the stove. Gram and James wanted some privacy so they could get to know each other better; so they went to bed, under the covers for warmth."

"What???" shouted Nina. "They weren't married or even thinking of marriage and they're allowed to go to bed together?"

"Wait, listen to this. *My Dad brought up a long board and sat it up between us. 'Stay on you own sides,' he told us. 'Mom and I are right outside in the next room.' We never touched all evening, but it was interesting.*"

"She writes that she was shy at first but they got to talking about his home life and about hers, about school, about friends. Here is another good one, I don't think Tom wants to hear this. *He is such a good talker. I could listen all night. The next thing I knew the board was being removed and James was thanking me for the lovely evening. He said he'd see me soon. His workday at the farm was tiring and he planned to get an early sleep tomorrow night in his own bed.*"

"Oh my God!" Nina gasped. "Should I write that?"

"I don't think so. Maybe we should tell him to read it himself. Let's start a code. How about IBNE, (interesting but not evidence). And then note the book and page numbers."

A horn sounded. Nina grabbed the sales slips and ran out to the gas pumps. Cary read on. When Nina came back, Cary was giggling.

"What's so funny? What I miss?"

"They didn't spend all their time in bed. *We went sliding on the hills on the snow. James's favorite phrase, when he fell down was 'oh Hokey!' Every time he fell off the sled it was 'Oh Hokey!"* That made me giggle for one thing. She writes so much about him, it's like I can see him. He's tall and muscular with dark brown curly hair, Just like BJ."

"Same first name too,"

Yeah, that brought Cary into her own thoughts; or was he a relative? Did they get married?

"Listen to this. *James is becoming a regular visitor, with the board in the bed. Last night, he reached over and held my hand. I was so thrilled,. I know I'm in love. When the weather warms up, we'll put on our warm coats and sit on the porch. I think we can sit even closer then.*"

"In the spring, planting a home garden took up several pages, the tilling of the soil, planting the seeds or sprouts they'd kept alive all winter in the house. The peach blossoms lent a beautiful color to the world and soon the peaches were ready to can. Gram and her mother evidently canned a lot of things for the next winter.

"Gram moaned into her diary that life seemed one cycle after another. The only bright spots were the visits from James. Listen to this. *He now talks a lot about the war we fought in Europe. He finds it hard to believe what the Nazi party was doing. His father got caught up in it. He never wanted to be a soldier and, later, a POW. But if it hadn't happened, I wouldn't have him with me! My parents have taken a shine to him even though he is German. Mom and Dad often invite James for Sunday dinner if he goes to church with us. Sometimes he misses church as there is so much work to do on his father's farm.*

Mom and Dad don't seem to mind that he's German. They said we have a little of that in our bloodline. They are good, strong, hard-working people, good providers, they said. Are they telling me that it's time I got married? I have to wait for James to ask me, but I do love being with him."

Nina sighed. "It's so real. Like we're there listening to her telling us what happened last night. She really pours her heart out. Can I get a diary? I'd have to backtrack on so much. I can picture my grandchildren wanting to read it."

"I have a couple empty diaries I'll never use. They're yours."

"I can't imagine going into a bed with a boy because it's cold outside. If I were that close, I'd rather cuddle. How do they deal with the cold?"

"I read that his father had a couple of bedpans that he filled with hot ash from the fireplace and put one in each side of the bed, to warm it up before they got in. Then they piled the covers on to keep it warm - covers that gram and her mother made. They didn't have stores like we do."

"He tells a lot of stories from other people in the community. A lot of them his father told him. Here's some real evidence. Double E," she told Nina.

"Americans found it hard to pronounce his last name, referring to his father, I think. *He was always called 'Huge' by his co-workers because he was big. So, when the farmer, my grandfather on my mother's side, had a chance, he legally helped him change his name from Huweylur to Huge. That's what people called him, so why not? He wanted to be an American."*

Nina gasped! "It is a relative of Tom. Spell that?"

"H-u-w-e-y-l-u-r"

H-u-w-e-y-l-u-r"

"I hope I spelled it right. But I have the book and the page. It may be evidence. What if they could find a prisoner with that name? Anything else interesting?"

"He talks a lot about when Hamlin was first settled. These are stories he got from his adoptive parents. The mother's relatives were here, then. They helped chop down trees and cut underbrush to make a road to the lake so other families could come and have land to settle on. She writes; '*The way ahead of them was so thick with trees, bushes, swamp and wild animals, that it come to be called the Black North.*'

"Wow, that's where the restaurant at Oak Orchard got its name." Nina remarked. Cary nodded, yes.

Cary proceeded to read. "*A group of men got together to cut a dirt road through the black north to the lake that they'd been told lay beyond the forest, not too far to the north. It would open more farmland for future people coming to Hamlin.*

"*They were fearful on the night before they left. Someone brought some homemade cider that they drank a good part of. almost didn't leave the next morning: so many were sick from too much cider. But they got started. Rumor has it that they imbibed a lot of cider on the way, also. That is why the road has so many curves, not a straight path.*"

They both laughed, knowing what they meant about Lake Road having curves.

"James had a sense of humor," Nina said. "And he was a good story teller. No wonder Gram liked him."

"Oh, wait, I think I found something very important. Give this book and page a double E. '*Several POW's from the camp worked on his adoptive father's farm. One guard came to watch over them. The first year went by with no trouble so the guards became lax and would take regular naps under a tree. One POW (my father) was making eyes with the farmer's daughter (his mother} and the day came when they disappeared into the forest, the POW and the girl.*

"*Winter came and the girl found she was pregnant. Her father thought it was all his fault for letting the POWs work the fields. He set to work trying to adopt the guy, get him out of camp to marry his daughter!*

"My heart skipped a beat. He was telling me something very personal about his family. The prisoner of war was very much in love with Jame's mother. He was scared to the core when the true Nazi in the camp tried to convince them all to rise up, revolt, because the Americans would kill them. This prisoner ran away with the guards chasing him!

'He threw his helmet and dogtags from the top of a hill into the lake. He hoped his child would find them and know he existed. Then the guards caught him.

He found out he was mistaken when they got him back to camp. They fed him, got him dry clothes, and were good to him. This got him in trouble with the other prisoners in the camp. It was very hard for him in the camp after that, now I know it was my father who run away! It all worked out. Dad got to stay and got adopted. They got married and here is my James."

Just then some visitors came in the marina channel. Their boat was flying Canadian flags. Visitors! Time to go back to work.

Cary set aside her book and got the necessary papers for visitors from another country to fill out. She'd find out where they were headed and let the ports along the American shore know who was coming and that they'd filled out the right papers.

CHAPTER FOURTEEN

BJ and Cindy had put the helmet and necklace to soak, locked the house, and left for his mother's house which was down County Line Rd a bit. It was hard for BJ to walk in - for maybe the last time - but it was a job that needed to be done. He pulled around to the back of the house and dropped the back hatch of the truck to make way for anything he decided he wanted to keep.

The sheriff had been there. The things from the dining room table were gone. Cindy got the broom because there were cigar wrappers on the floor.

"Wait," BJ told her. "Tom and I did some research last night on cigar bands. Did you know people collect them?"

"I wouldn't have thought of that. But the brand is probably a clue as to who was here," Cindy answered.

"I hope the sheriff kept a few. Maybe there are fingerprints on them. Let's see if Mom has any plastic bags in the cupboard and some tweezers. We'll keep these for a while."

"Do you feel like you're in a detective mystery show?"

"Yeah," he laughed. "Amazing what good things you can learn from TV."

BJ turned to go down the basement stairs. "Hey! Look what I found!" He held up a round wooden tub with a crank on it. "Can't hold it long, This guy's heavy!"

Coming to the top of the stairs to see, Cindy asked, "What's that?"

"That thing made some of the best ice cream around. I'm bringing it home. We're making our own ice cream!"

"Okay, but can we keep this dining room set? I know just the place for it in our house."

BJ came back up, throwing the ice cream maker in his truck.

"The tables awful dark."

"A good cleaning will bring it back to life, and our living room end tables just might match it. We could always paint it. I just love the lines."

"You up to helping me hoist it into the back of the truck?"

"Absolutely - and the china cabinet, too? We can put the ping pong table in the basement."

"So long as we keep the ping pong set somewhere," replied BJ. "I did a lot of homework on this table. Tom did too. We might have to sand some scratches out of the wood."

"Oh yeah," Cindy joked, "I see 1+1=2"

BJ gave her a mean look. (As mean as he could muster.)

"How about that floor lamp? I can see Mom working under it now."

"I think so. I was thinking of trying my hand at sewing. That would work well over a sewing machine."

"What are you going to sew?"

"You never know when a little one might come along."

"Are you telling me something?"

"No, not yet. But someday."

"I'm ready if you are." He stroked her cheek. "Maybe I'd better get some men to help me carry the heavy pieces out."

"Maybe you should," she laughed. "One good thing, BJ, when it happens, we've got three built-in babysitters. Cary, Nina, and Tom."

"Not all of them together!" he joked. "You got the cigar bands?" He asked. She nodded yes.

"Then let's look upstairs. Let's give the girls and Mrs. Travers first choice before we set a date for the furniture sale."

"Sounds good to me, so long as you and Tom get first choice: for instance, like the ice cream maker," she laughed.

"Do you think it's a good idea to have those girls reading Mom's diary?"

"What do you know of your mom's life before you were born?"

"Not much, actually. They always lived in this house. I think it was a family house before then. But the details of her childhood? No, not a clue."

"Most people don't know their history, but their parents had lives, and things happened to shape them into who they became. It might be very informative. I didn't know your mom, I'm sorry to say. My mom had anger issues and a strictness I thought was beyond necessary. I was a good kid. If she'd kept a diary, maybe I'd understand her more. I could forgive her for a couple of things that always bothered me."

"My mom was next to perfect as you can get, except for dying early."

Wanting to change the subject back to the fun they'd been having Cindy remarked, "I bet they're laughing away in heaven at the old-fashioned things they're reading. They'd have lots of stories for us to laugh at today."

BJ's phone rang. "It's Cary. Hi!" He listened for a while. "Thanks Cary. Mark that page!"

"What now?" Cindy asked

"They found an entry where granddad told about his father's escape from camp and throwing his helmet and dog tags into the water."

"OMG! That's why he came to Tom in the dream. Tom was meant to find them!"

CHAPTER FIFTEEN

Tom waved goodbye to Judge Travers. The sun was bright. A lot of people should show up today.

Oh, he thought, I haven't heard about a sailing class tomorrow. I wonder if it's still on. He went into the office and called Chief Garret at the Coast Guard Station.

"Garrett speaking," came the brisk answer.

"Hi. This is Tom Huge at Braddock's. Just wondering if you needed me for the sailing class tomorrow?"

"So sorry! No one called you? I know how busy you are. Seaman Gary will take tomorrow's class. We need you there at Braddock's Bay for one more week. New people will stop in there today, and maybe all of next week, to get acquainted with the operation. I know you'll train them well for us. Make sure they know how to use the equipment. I hear good things about your effort there."

"It's been a pleasure, Chief. I look forward to meeting them. Are they local?"

"No, their main operation is on Canandaigua Lake."

Two men walked into the office. "Glad to be of help, Chief. Got a customer! Bye now"

"I'm Tom. How can I help you?"

"We're from Canandaigua. The chief said he'd let you know we were coming."

"Yes, that was just him. Want to take a look around?"

Just then, a horn honked on the dock for pumpouts.

"Good way to get started," one of the guys joked. "My name is Arny, by the way, and my friend, here, is Stan."

Stan stuck out his hand. "Didn't know our instructor would be so young."

"I grew up on a marina, west of here. We'll probably be working together a lot. My Uncle BJ is usually here, but I'll show you what I can - tell you some of the idiosyncrasies of the boaters. We've got a sailboat in the slings right now. It's a rush job for the Coast Guard. Chad, the fiberglass guy should be finished repairing the damage today. We'll see if we can put it back into the water soon. Another nice job for you."

"BJ's Marina. I've heard of it. You do a lot of rescue work and motor repair. Glad to get to know you." They walked together out to the pump-out station. Stan picked up the hose while the boat's owner made sure everything electric was turned off and the guy was out of the boat.

Arny spoke up. "I think your downriggers are still connected."

The boat's owners jumped back into the boat and flipped that switch. "Good catch. Thanks a lot."

Stan was sniffing the air. "I smell smoke and it's not from this boat." They all looked around. Stan pointed to Sam Sander's boat. "I think that guy is relaxing with a cigar. No big deal but you have to be careful."

Tom thought to himself that these guys would be all right. At the same time, the hairs on his head seemed to stand up. Cigars!

"You've got this. I need to speak to that guy anyway. If I'm still there when you're done, come over and I'll introduce you."

The captain of the boat having its head pumped exchanged a look with Tom. Stan and Arny didn't miss it, Tom explained. "He's kind of infamous but he's here to enjoy his boat. He's been nothing but helpful to me. BJ says to treat him like any other boater and just get through the season."

"Good morning."

Tom surprised him as Sam quickly stamped out his cigar. "Love the smell of cigars. My grandfather smoked them and collected cigar bands. This brings back good memories," Tom lied. "What brand is that?"

Sam dug out his cigar and showed Tom the band.

"We seem to be kindred spirits." Sam remarked. "You don't find many cigar lovers today. My father smoked this brand, so I've always stuck with it. Never found any reason to change."

"Just wanted to tell you that I'll only be here one more week. The bosses found someone to run this marina. They'll be over in a few minutes and I'll introduce you. I wanted to thank you for all the help you've given me. It's been a pleasure to get to know you the way I do."

"Good luck to you, boy. You give me hope for the next generation. I see too much bad. You embody nothing but good! It's been my pleasure to get to know you."

The two new caretakers approached. Tom made the introductions, then hurried away as the others stayed to talk about boats.

Once in the office, Tom called BJ. "You won't believe it, but Sam Sanders smokes cigars, The same brand that we found in Gram's house."

"Oh, Hokey," BJ replied.

"What's that mean?" asked Tom.

"When our two girls were reading my mother's diary, that swear word came up! Now everything is Oh, hokey! Can you get a cigar band from him? It might be evidence."

"Yeah, I told him my father smoked the same kind of cigar and collected the bands. Maybe he thinks I want a newer version to add to the collection!"

"Oh, hokey, Tom. You're getting to be quite the storyteller."

"And you're absolutely silly. Oh, hokey back at you."

"Well, thanks for the news, This just gets more and more interesting. Got to get back to the furniture moving. I don't know where we'll put all this stuff, but we're having fun."

"Oh, wait. We've been replaced. The new caretakers are here now. Chief Garrett said one more week to train them. They're both a lot older than me. More like you, old man!"

"Oh, hokey, get back to work!! This is actually good news. These girls are driving me crazy with their updates from Mom, as they call it. They find a lot to laugh at in the stories Mom told. Can't wait to read them myself. I don't see how Mom's life could be so different than mine. Guess I'll find out. One interesting thing! They said not to throw away anything German. I always saw the souvenirs from when they visited there, but I didn't think they had any special meaning other than memories of a nice vacation. Cary says I may be surprised."

"See you later. I've got to make sure the new guys can run the travel lift. The fiberglass guy is done and says we can launch the sailboat later today. Not as much damage as we thought. Just a lot of rubbing from the rocks and a couple of small cracks. Gary will be happy. I'll call him when we're done talking."

"My boss is anxious to load some things onto the truck so I'll see you later. I could use your help moving things. You can work on building some muscles. Oh! I saved Mom's old ice cream maker. That'll build muscles!"

"Great, I'll see how these guys handle the travel lift, launching Gary's sailboat. Assuming all goes well, I'll be right home. I can't wait to see the things you're finding at Gram's house and read what the girls found in her diary."

"See if you can leave early enough to drive the boat home. Then we're almost moved back here. The judge will gladly drive you back and forth, I think."

"I've got to invite Cary to the movies this weekend."

"That too," BJ said.

CHAPTER SIXTEEN

Gary and Sam were chatting at the local park. They often had their talks there at a secluded table. Gary didn't want to be seen hanging out with a mafia guy. Sam understood. Gary had a squeaky clean image to maintain, so he joined the Coast Guard. He never mentioned his family connections when he joined. He knew being unrecognized as a family member would come in handy some day. If Sam went to jail, no one would suspect Gary, the Coast Guard guy, of being involved.

"The wiretapping device I got you - has it paid off?" Sam asked.

"I installed it. Nothing yet. But I'm also recording BJ's and Tom's conversations so I don't miss anything. You didn't buy it yourself?"

"No! I've been around long enough to know better than that. The wife of one of my guys picked it up from a friend. My name was never mentioned. My guy's not a snitch."

"Well I hope so. I was able to put it on the office phone. We should have got the home phone too. Wait, something's going on! Listen!"

They listened in as plans were made for Cary, Tom, Cindy and BJ to make believe, for Cary's sake, that they were going on a double date Saturday night. BJ and Tom talked about a surprise party for Cary's birthday back at the marina, how Cindy was going to play sick so they'd have to come right back home. Her whole school class would be waiting to help celebrate. There would be a band playing, lots of fun.

"That's great!" said Gary. "We can keep them down at the parking lot while we search the house."

Sam lit up with an idea. "Isn't Central School their rival?"

"What are you thinking?"

"I know some kids there. Let's get word to them to crash the party and cause some trouble! That will give us some more time."

"Give them some money to take a couple of kegs of beer along," Gary suggested. "I know BJ and Tom found the treasure at Devil's Nose. I don't know how they even knew it was there. But that last time when I saw the four of them dragging a motor out of the water, I had a feeling something was up. I never saw a more suspicious bunch in my life! Those girls were actually shaking! And they haven't been back there nosing around since."

"We'll meet down the road a bit and watch them leave, then go straight to the house and see if we can find anything that looks like valuable centuries old treasure."

"With our granddad's name on it."

CHAPTER SEVENTEEN

"Cary, BJ, and Cindy are going to the movies in town on Saturday. Would you like to go with me?" Tom asked Cary when they were alone.

"I should ask what's playing - but sure I'll go. What's playing?"

"No idea. Just thought it might be fun, like a date if we were older."

"Oh! It's my birthday. Let me ask my Mom if it's okay. She might have something else planned."

"Give her a call right now! Then I can tell BJ and Cindy."

Cary picked up the office phone and called her mom.

"Mom, I know Saturday is my birthday but Tom asked me to go to the movies with him. Can I go? BJ and Cindy are also going."

She listened for a minute. She could hear her mom talking to the judge.

"Great, Mom. Yes, it's a nice way to celebrate my birthday. Thanks." She gave Tom a great big smile.

"Mom said it's okay with them."

"It's your birthday, so I'd better make it special." Tom knew just the thing: a pink flowered bracelet. He had to find time to shop.

*****

Saturday night, Nina waved bye, saying not to worry about the marina. She and the judge would man the radio and gas pump until they got back. If anyone got in trouble out there, the coast guard would have to handle it - or the local auxiliary.

Cary loved the bracelet Tom found for her. This would be fun!

Unfortunately, they got to the theater too early, so they sat in a soda shop and had a soda.

Back at the marina, Judge Travers used the boat hauler to get a flat top hay wagon in place at the edge of the parking lot for the band who were already arriving. He had made an announcement at school that went to everyone but Cary, that a secret birthday bash was scheduled; they were all invited to the marina after seven p.m.

Seaman Gary happened to stop as he was driving by and the Judge asked him to leave. This was a high school event; no adults were allowed. Gary left.

Mrs. Travers stamped the students' hands and offered sodas and chips. She had a salad, hot dogs, and cake for later.

The band was good and loud! The dancing had started when BJ, Cindy, Tom and Cary pulled back into the driveway.

"You fooled me!" Shouted Cary over the roar. "My first date ruined, but Wow! Thank you for fooling me! They're all here - all my class!"

"Mrs. Travers is guarding the door and will switch to serving party food when they're all here."

"You all fooled me!"

"Well, you got me last year." BJ reminded her. "Go have fun!"

Tom and Cary went to join a giggling Nina.

"All these people! How'd you all do this without my knowing?" Cary asked.

"You did kind of have your nose in a book lately," Tom replied. "This should be fun. I get to kiss the birthday girl."

Kisses! Then all the guys seemed to leave their dates to line up behind Tom. "I've never been kissed - and now a couple of hundred at one time?" Cary shook her head!

"There's not this many in our class. Tom, some of these kids I don't know!"

Tom stopped one boy he didn't know.

"What school do you go to?"

"I heard about the party from a friend. I'm from Central High. There's a bunch of us here and we have beer over by the red car."

Cary turned away from him. "I don't know him."

She turned to Tom, "I'm worried, a lot of these kids I don't know."

Just then a fight broke out. These were rival schools!

"Tom, let's go up to the house and tell the adults. I think that I smelled alcohol on that boy. Maybe we have to stop this!"

Mrs. Travers spoke up. "The adults are in the office. By the way, Seaman Gary stopped by before, but the Judge sent him away."

"Is he the German dream soldier I expected at Cary's party?" Tom mused aloud. They both looked at him strangely.

"My last dream was about a party for Cary and the German soldier showing up."

Nina disappeared and came back with BJ and the Judge. BJ whispered to Tom, "Take it easy; the police are on their way. We need to keep these guys all here so we can get to the bottom of this."

Soon the sound of sirens could be heard above the music. The kids tried to scatter, but the road into the marina back lot had been blocked. Someone had mysteriously moved the 'beast' across the road. With the music playing, no one even heard it start up.

BJ went to the musicians and quietly told them to pack up and get ready to leave. The party was over and the road would be unblocked when the sheriff got there.

Then he took a flare gun from the nearest boat and made a run for the house, sensing something more was going on.

Tom and one of the sheriffs, with a real gun followed BJ to the house. They entered by both doors, blocking anyone trying to leave.

BJ switched on the lights as he went. Tom and the sheriff stayed put, covering the doors until they knew something definite.

They could hear voices in the basement.

"All this stuff looks old. Oh yeah, they're clearing out the old family house getting it ready to sell. "

"Maybe we should buy it. It's been a good hideout."

"When we find the treasure, we can buy anything," Sam said.

Gary snorted! "I thought you wanted it for its sentimental value!"

"Some people will believe anything!"

"If I'm not getting to keep it on my shelf, I'm not helping you find it!"

"Sh... I think it's in this safe here." He tossed the blanket aside which covered the safe.

"Amateurs! We found it right away."

"How are you at safe cracking?" Gary asked.

"My only thought would be to blow it up. Let's see if we can move it out and blow it elsewhere."

"But that would ruin the treasure!"

"Take it easy. I know a guy. They'll hear you over the music. Wait, the music stopped. Must be taking a break."

"And a swig of beer," Gary replied.

They tried to tug the safe onto the blanket and tow it toward the basement door.

"How will we get it up in the car?" Gary asked.

"Stop sniveling! Can't you see I'm thinking?"

Suddenly Sam felt a gun in his back. He noticed Gary standing there with his hands up.

BJ and Tom came running from their positions at the front door.

"So, you found our safe. Let's leave it right there! Take a seat on the couches! Why are you so intent on getting this safe? You think we have money?"

Just then the Judge, Mrs. Travers, Nina, and Cary came in the basement door; they also took seats.

"What's going on down at the party?" BJ asked.

Cary spoke up, "The cops have the two sides separated. The ones from our school were allowed to call their parents to come get them. The others are being questioned as to how they found out about the party and who brought the beer. The musicians are gone."

Tom put his arm around Cary.

"I'm sorry your party got ruined."

"It's not your fault! Just between the two of us, Cindy said I should force you to make it up to me."

That brought a smile all around except for Gary and Sam, who weren't smiling.

"Okay, Sam, what has this got to do with you? Why are you so interested in what we found at Devil's Nose? That is what you're after, isn't it?"

"The treasure you found belongs to Gary's and my family."

"You're related?" A surprised sheriff choked out.

"Open the safe. I'll tell you what I think is in it." Sam said.

BJ opened the safe to reveal nothing. The safe was empty.

"I see, okay, but I'm sure we weren't wasting our time. That morning at the Nose, when you pulled the boat off the beach, you found something, didn't you."

Gary finally spoke up. "What did you do with the treasure that belongs to us?"

Cindy said. "Try looking in that wash tub over there."

Gary went over and pulled out the helmet and dog tags. He looked at it with wonder.

"They really exist! There's our ancestor's name, Huweylur, and his number."

BJ was twisting in his seat. "What do you mean, your ancestor?"

"The story has been handed down in our family that he escaped from the POW camp. Just as he thought he was going to be captured and killed, he threw those things into the lake. He hoped his children would someday find them and know he didn't run away from them. Sam and I are cousins and we've been searching for them for a long time!"

"One mystery has been solved! His girlfriend was pregnant. That's why he was allowed to live and become an American," BJ said.

"How did you know about them?" Sam asked.

Cary spoke up. "We've been reading BJ's mother's diaries. Her husband, when they were dating, told the story of his father being a prisoner of war. He was convinced by the real Nazis in the camp that he was about to die. He had a girlfriend on the farm that he was working on and, well, she got pregnant! He did escape - but then he got caught. His new father-in-law sponsored him and kept him in this country rather than see his daughter's heartbreak."

"Does that mean that we're all relatives?" Sam asked eagerly.

"Tom's ancestor did almost get killed. And he had a sense of humor!" Cary added.

They all looked at Tom who was about to spill more beans into this real bowl of historic soup.

"He came to me in my dreams! I saw him throw the helmet into the lake. That's how I knew which direction to look. It was off the west side of the Nose. He told me to get out of his dream."

They all laughed. "Then he came and told me that the Germans would be at the party tonight."

BJ spoke up, "Now that we all know how weird you are, Tom..."

"No! I believe him," Gary said. "I've been having dreams of a German soldier also. But I never thought to follow the direction of the helmet throw. Truthfully, it was a story handed down in both our families, Sam and mine."

"BJ figured the directions out. We went up to where I was in my dream and reenacted the throw. You were looking in the wrong place."

Sam was shaking his head.

"I never believed Gary's dreams. Guess I'd better work on having some of my own dreams; like, where did Mugsy Seigel hide his stash from the Las Vegas Strip?" That brought a laugh to them all.

Gary, running his fingers over the dog tags and showing them to Sam, spoke.

"Now the question is, what do we do with them? They obviously belong to all of us, and they might be worth a lot of money. Also, I hear there is a foundation that collects German dog tags."

Judge Traver's wife spoke up. We have a small private museum here in Hamlin. How about donating the helmet, tags, and story to them? Then we can visit them any time we want."

"It sounds good to me - but Gary wanted something to put on his shelf," Sam said.

"And I want to read those diaries," Gary said.

"I know the museum curator. I'm sure she'll arrange for a fancy plaque to thank Gary for his gift. Then we can all visit the items whenever we want."

Tom was still looking puzzled.

"We're all related?"

"Seems like we're all on the same side," BJ said.

"Sorry to use your family house for a hideout. I'm truly drawn to the family history within it's walls. How much do you want for it?" Gary asked.

"I want enough to get Tom through college and a little more for the worry you caused us," BJ replied.

"Done! What do you want to study?" Gary asked Tom.

"I guess the natural thing is some kind of investigative work," Tom replied.

"You should be good at that, with the help of your dreams. Proud to have you in the family."

"What about you, Sam? Will I be putting you in jail someday?" Tom asked.

"He's all bark and no bite, as the old saying goes. I'll keep him in line!" This is from the Coast Guard man, Gary.

NOTES AND AUTHOR'S OTHER BOOKS

Notes from the author: many of these stories can be found in the Hamlin, NY library in the book
"Remembering Hamlin," by Mary E. Smith.

Forgive me, Ms. Smith for the liberties and exaggerations I took. The story of the soldier
throwing his helmet off Devil's Nose was purely fiction. The POW camp is real and can be
visited on Moscow Rd, just east of the entrance to Hamlin Beach State Park. One of the stories I
got from Mrs. Smith's book involved the building of the roads to the lake. Left out was an
interesting story about the Ho-jack line. Also, the town may have been named after the first vice-
president to Lincoln! Others thought it was named after a town in Germany. It would be nice to
see which version is correct. You might want to read these and the other firsthand stories Mrs.
Smith collected.

Another interesting place to visit is The Hamlin Historical Center 864 WalkerLake Ontario Rd.
Call first at 585-964-7385 or email historian@hamlin,ny.org

Other books by the author;
Overboard in Lake Ontario, first in this series
Biblical Dream Study – takes dreams in the Bible and finds interpretation messages for us.
Finding Spirit in Prison Inmate's Dreams – three years teaching them to understand what God was telling them in their dreams. You'll find many insights into understanding your own
dreams.
He's Not Gone – dreams around the time of her husband's passing. Proof life goes on.
God's Golden Sword as seen in My Dreams For Others – Ever wish you could have a two-
way conversation with your creator? This book, a memoir, showa you how.
Me? Start a Dream Group? Directions on the why and how of starting a group with many
suggestions to understanding your own dreams.
All available on Amazon, your local library or loc